Thank you for your consideration

Michelle
GOES TO
Congress

M. Moray

Published By: Pen Legacy®

Illustration & Formatting By: India Sheana

Edited By: U Can Mark My Word Editorial Services

Library of Congress Cataloging – in- Publication Data has been applied for.

ISBN: 978-1-7366118-6-9

PRINTED IN THE UNITED STATES OF AMERICA.

"Good morning, boys and girls! Today is our field trip to Washington D.C. to visit Congress," Mr. Cauley told the students. "By the time I finish taking attendance, the school bus should be here."

"Welcome to the U.S. Capitol Building, home of the United States Congress! As we enter the building, please be quiet as the members are in session and the legislative aides and other staffers are working. You are allowed to ask questions during the tour, but please stay with the group and do not wander off."

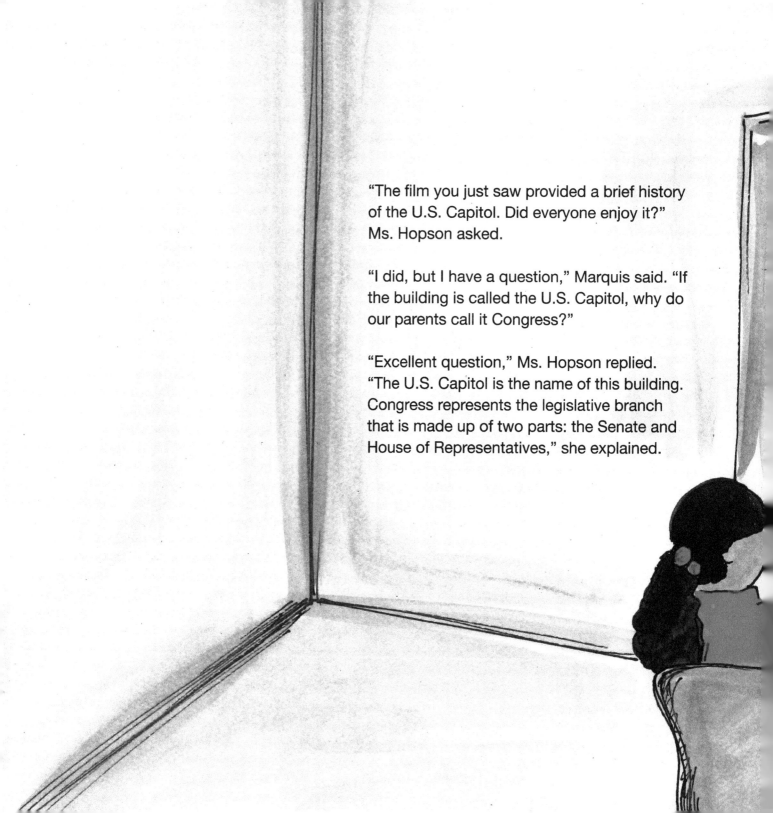

"The film you just saw provided a brief history of the U.S. Capitol. Did everyone enjoy it?" Ms. Hopson asked.

"I did, but I have a question," Marquis said. "If the building is called the U.S. Capitol, why do our parents call it Congress?"

"Excellent question," Ms. Hopson replied. "The U.S. Capitol is the name of this building. Congress represents the legislative branch that is made up of two parts: the Senate and House of Representatives," she explained.

Welcome
to the
US Capitol

"This section of the U.S. Capitol is called the Rotunda. Does anyone know what it is used for?" Ms. Hopson asked.

All the children raised their hands.

"It is where state funerals are held for presidents, Congress members, military heroes, and other honored people, "Arnold answered.

"That's correct! You are a smart bunch, but let me see who knows this," Ms. Hopson told the group. "Which former president was supposed to be buried here but never was, and his empty tomb lies two stories below the Rotunda?"

"George Washington," Michelle answered.

"Can we go see it?" Leon asked.

"Not today," Mr. Cauley told him. "However, we will continue the tour with Ms. Hopson."

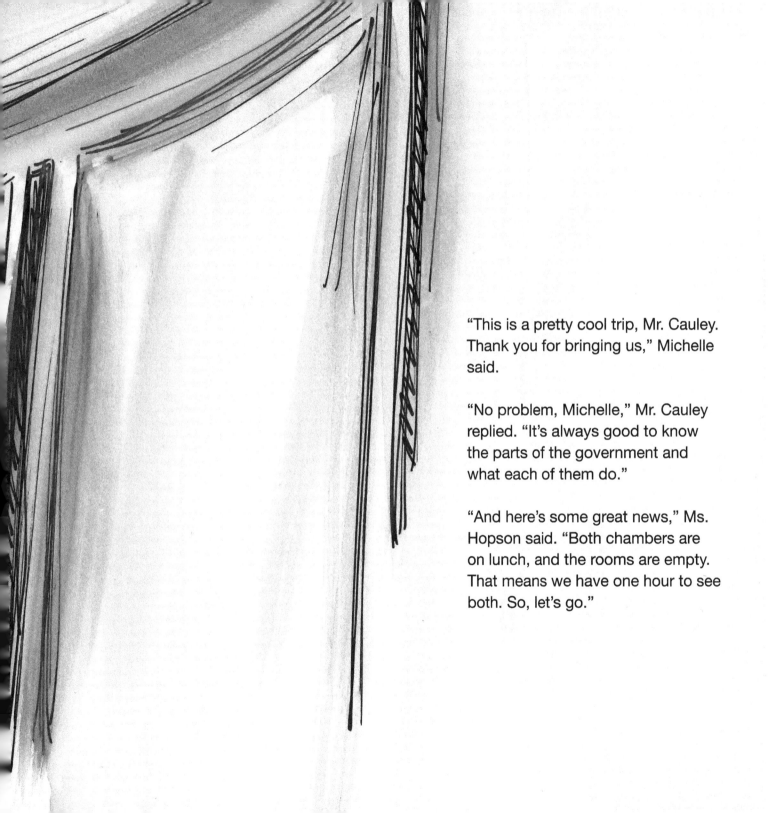

"This is a pretty cool trip, Mr. Cauley. Thank you for bringing us," Michelle said.

"No problem, Michelle," Mr. Cauley replied. "It's always good to know the parts of the government and what each of them do."

"And here's some great news," Ms. Hopson said. "Both chambers are on lunch, and the rooms are empty. That means we have one hour to see both. So, let's go."

"Welcome to the chambers where the House of Representatives meet and handle all government business," Ms. Hopson said.

"What exactly does the House of Representatives do?" Steven asked.

"The primary responsibility of the House of Representatives is to create new laws and make changes to existing laws, which are written as bills," Ms. Hopson explained. "They are the lower house but the closest to the people since they represent districts within each state, giving you a total of 435 voting representatives."

"Oh wow! Mrs. Nancy is the Speaker of the House. My mom told me that the Speaker is a very important person," Michelle said.

"Your mother is right. The Speaker of the House is the second in the United States presidential line of succession after the vice president. That means, if anything happened to the president and vice president where they couldn't carry out their duties, the Speaker would become the president," Ms. Hopson told the children.

"How is the House speaker elected?" Marquis asked. "By the majority of the representatives from the party with the most members at the beginning of the new congressional year," Ms. Hopson replied. "You guys are asking great questions. Let's head over to the Senate's chamber before they return from lunch."

"This is the home of the Senate. Some people often refer to the Senate as 'checkers' because they normally confirm or approve actions done by the House or President. This is by far the most important chamber," Ms. Hopson said. "So, when the House wants to pass a bill, they have to get it approved by the Senate before it can become a law?" Steven asked.

"That's right. The House creates bills to help the American people. Then those bills are sent to the Senate for a majority vote and forwarded to the president to sign," Ms. Hopson replied.

"My mommy said our government runs better when the same party controls both the House and the Senate," Isreal said.

"Yes, especially since the parties don't always want to help and serve all people," Catherine added.

"Other than denying bills or giving the House a hard time, what else does the Senate do?" Marquis asked.

Ms. Hopson laughed at his comment before responding.

"They don't give the House a hard time. They were created to protect the rights of individual states. They are comprised of two senators from each state, totaling one hundred senators for the fifty states. They are responsible for the approval of treaties and the confirmation of cabinet secretaries, Supreme Court Justices, federal judges, and other federal executive officials," Ms. Hopson said.

"So they have fewer members but the most power?" Steven asked, looking confused.
"I wouldn't say they have more power. They are just responsible for more of the verifying and confirming, which is a responsibility many don't like them to have," Ms. Hopson responded.
"I have a trivia for you, Ms. Hopson," Michelle said.

"Oh really? Okay, whatcha got?" Ms. Hopson said.

"Congress is the only one elected directly by the people. True or false?" Michelle asked her. Without hesitating, Ms. Hopson replied, "True. The electoral college elects the President. The Supreme Court is nominated by the President and confirmed by the Senate, but the American people elect Congress during elections," she explained.

"That's right, Ms. Hopson!" Michelle said.

"Boy, you are a smart group of children! Mr. Cauley, you are doing a great job teaching them history," Ms. Hopson commented.

"We do our best. Plus, with the state of the country and this last election, our government, democracy, and what that all means have been a major topic of discussion," Mr. Cauley told her.

"I must say I am truly impressed with all of you interested in our government. Keep up the good work. Now, before you go off to lunch, are there any final questions for me?" Ms. Hopson asked.

"Yes," Marie said. "Which one of the three branches is most important?"

"Well, Congress is the most important, with the Supreme Court coming in a close second. I say that because Congress is responsible for making laws that influence our daily lives. They also declare war, conduct investigations, control spending and taxing powers, and serve as the voice of the people and the states in the federal government. Their decisions are binding, and once their decision becomes a law, it can only be amended. However, the law is forever. The Supreme Court is responsible for making sure the laws created follow the laws and rights to the people within the Constitution," Hopson said.

"Well, children, thank Ms. Hopson for her time," Mr. Cauley said.

"Thank you, Ms. Hopson," the children responded in unison.

"Wait, Ms. Hopson, I have one final trivia," Michelle said.

"Okay. Whatcha got for me?" Ms. Hopson said.

"What is the name of the statue that sits on top of this building?" Michelle asked.

"I have no clue," Ms. Hopson replied, pretending not to know the answer so she could see if Michelle would get it right.

"The Statue of Freedom," Michelle told her.

"Thanks for sharing, Michelle. I swear you children are the best! Have an amazing rest of the day," Ms. Hopson said as the children left the U.S. Capitol Building. "Thank you for visiting Congress!"

"Don't Boo, VOTE"
~ Former President Barack Obama

The Constitutional Amendments
Pertaining to Voting

Amendment 15

"The right of citizens of the United States to vote shall not be denied or abridged by the United States or by any State on account of race, color, or previous condition of servitude." (Passed by Congress February 26, 1869. Ratified February 3, 1870)

Amendment 19

"The right of citizens of the United States to vote shall not be denied or abridged by the United States or by any State on account of sex." (Passed by Congress June 4, 1919. Ratified August 18, 1920)

Amendment 24

"The right of citizens of the United States to vote in any primary or other election for President or Vice President, for electors for President or Vice President, or for Senator or Representative in Congress, shall not be denied or abridged by the United States or any State by reason of failure to pay poll tax or other tax." (Passed by Congress August 27, 1962. Ratified January 23, 1964)

Amendment 26

"The right of citizens of the United States, who are eighteen years of age or older, to vote shall not be denied or abridged by the United States or by any State on account of age." (Passed by Congress March 23, 1971. Ratified July 1, 1971.)

In 2021, Americans Are Fighting To Keep Their Right To Vote.... The Voting Saga Continues!

More Books In The Michelle Children's Series

www.charronmonaye.com